PLAY BY PLAY
BASEBALL

Coach Don Geng, Coach Steve
Scherber, and the following athletes
were photographed for this book:
  A.J. Capewell,
  Matt Cavanaugh,
  John Dittberner,
  Ben Doran,
  Blake Dotson,
  Christian Edwards,
  Mike Griffin,
  Brandon Hammergren,
  Kathryn Hetherington,
  Michael Honsa,
  Jay Johnson,
  Mike Killeen,
  Dan Lewer,
  Tony Liuzzi,
  Melissa Peterson,
  Dave Shelley,
  Andy Williams,
  Rob Worthington.

LERNER
SPORTS
AN IMPRINT OF LERNER PUBLISHING GROUP

PLAY BY PLAY
BASEBALL

Don Geng
Photographs by Andy King

Lerner Publications Company ● Minneapolis

To all my mentors who have continued to be inspirations: My coaches for whom I've played and served, my teachers, and my parents.

LernerSports
An imprint of Lerner Publishing Group
241 First Avenue North
Minneapolis, MN 55401 U.S.A.

Website address: www.lernerbooks.com

Library of Congress Cataloging-in-Publication Data

Geng, Don.
    Play-by-play Baseball / Don Geng ;
photographs by Andy King.
        p.   cm.
    Rev. ed. of: Fundamental baseball. ©1995.
    Includes bibliographical references and index.
    Summary: Presents information on the history of baseball and the equipment used, demonstrates the basic skills involved in fielding, throwing, hitting, and baserunning, and describes how these skills are used in a game.
    ISBN 0-8225-9880-9 (pbk. : alk. paper)
    1. Baseball—Juvenile literature. [1. Baseball.] I. King, Andy, ill. II. Geng, Don. Fundamental baseball. III. Title.
GV867.5.G46 2001
796.357—dc21   00-008879

Manufactured in the United States of America
1 2 3 4 5 6 – GPS – 06 05 04 03 02 01

Photo Acknowledgments
Photographs are reproduced with the permission of: pp. 7, 13 (top), Toronto Blue Jays; pp. 9, 10 (top), Independent Picture Service; p. 10 (bottom), Courtesy of the Boston Public Library, Print Department; pp. 11 (both), 13 (bottom), National Baseball Hall of Fame and Museum, Cooperstown, N.Y.; p. 12, John Doman/St. Paul Pioneer Press; p. 25, Gregory Drezdzon/Seattle Mariners.

CONTENTS

A NOTE FROM PAUL MOLITOR

Since I began playing at the age of five, baseball has given me a great life. I have had the thrills of being on teams that were St. Paul (Minnesota) City Champs at St. Luke's Grade School, state champions at Attucks Brooks American Legion and Cretin High School, Big Ten champs at the University of Minnesota, and World Champions for the Toronto Blue Jays. But more important than all of these championships have been the great friends, experiences, and memories. Your own friendships, experiences, and even championships, will become a part of you as your love for the game grows.

But a love of the game doesn't just happen—you have to have the desire to give your best effort whenever you play baseball, whether it's in the backyard, black-topped playground, street, or manicured playing diamond. You have to believe in yourself, like the early 1900s player Wee Willie Keeler did. Only 5 feet, 4 inches tall and 140 pounds, Willie still has the fifth highest lifetime batting average in the history of major league baseball. You have to believe that nothing will stop you—not size, not background, not coaching, not equipment.

Is believing in yourself easy? It wasn't for me. I remember crying, sulking, and going off by myself when I had a bad game or made a bad play at a crucial time. How can you avoid these negative emotions?

Set goals, long term and short term. Commit yourself to the idea that you will work harder than anyone. You will listen better, practice the details, and never get discouraged. You will set short-term goals like, "I'll get a hit next time," or "I'll take 50 extra swings in my basement."

Try to learn by watching and imitating the most successful players, whether they are your teammates, local stars, or a favorite pro player. Here's what I do. I take out a videotape of Tony Gwynn and watch him hit over and over until I memorize his style. Then I practice in my mind, trying to see myself become Tony, imitating his success. Then I go into the batting cage and try to copy his quiet hands and patience at the plate. I try to wait until the last second and rocket a line drive to the opposite field the way Tony does. Try this technique—it works!

If you're lucky, you'll have as many great coaches as I did, and a parent or another family member who encourages and supports you. However, you

Paul Molitor was the Most Valuable Player in the 1993 World Series. The Toronto Blue Jays won, thanks to Paul's outstanding play. In 1996, Paul joined the Minnesota Twins. He played for the Twins until he retired after the 1998 season. Molitor joined the Twins as a coach in the 1999 season.

may not be so lucky as to have everything go your way. Don't let this stop you. Great players have come from disadvantaged backgrounds. Who knows? You may be the next star!

As you improve, keep humble and keep striving to become better. Don't become cocky or too satisfied with your success. Perhaps my pet peeve is "trash talking"—the players who strut after a home run or who taunt a strikeout victim. In my opinion, this behavior has no place in baseball.

Finally, play hard, but play cleanly and within the rules of the game. Play and practice wholeheartedly, with as much enthusiasm as you have.

I wish each and every one of you success in both baseball and your life. Commit yourself to a goal and strive to reach it. Have fun and take pleasure in your efforts. Take care and God bless!

Paul Molitor
Eighth all–time leader with 3,319 hits

Chapter 1

HOW THIS GAME GOT STARTED

The fascinating history of baseball reflects the development of America itself. Although baseball has seen many changes, more has remained thesame than has changed.

The game has always involved two teams playing on a large field on which there are four bases. The teams take turns trying to hit a ball with a bat and playing in the field. A player on the team at bat tries to hit a ball thrown by one of the players on the fielding team. If the ball is hit, the batter tries to score a run by touching all the bases. The fielders' objective is to prevent the batter's team from scoring runs.

Baseball may have evolved from a game called rounders that was popular in England during the 1600s. As in baseball, a player hit a ball with a bat and ran around four bases. Unlike baseball, the players in the field

This woodcut illustration from Robin Carver's 1834 book, Book of Sports, *shows children playing rounders.*

Alexander Cartwright

threw the ball at the runner to prevent a score. American colonists in the 1700s played rounders, but they began to call the game "base ball."

Until the mid-1800s, baseball was played by different rules in different areas. Some historians believe that players in New York City made the most significant rule change in the 1830s or 1840s when they began touching the runner with the ball in their hands (a **tag**), rather than throwing the ball at the runner. In 1845, Alexander Cartwright wrote a rulebook for the sport. According to his rulebook, players made a **putout** by tagging a runner, and the distance between bases was set at 90 feet.

Baseball evolved throughout the 1800s. In 1859, a rule was adopted to end a game after 9 **innings** if one team had more runs than the other. Before that, teams played until one

The Knickerbocker Nine were members of Alexander Cartwright's Base Ball Club of New York.

team had 21 runs. Players could pitch overhand after an 1884 rule change.

Baseball grew in popularity in the late 1800s, both during and after the Civil War. Soldiers from all over the United States learned the game from Northern soldiers who played baseball during breaks in the fighting. In 1869, the Cincinnati Red Stockings' owners paid all their baseball players, making them the first professionals. The National League began in 1876 with eight pro teams. Five other leagues sprang up briefly to compete with the National League but all failed until the American League was formed in 1901. Three more leagues failed after 1901.

Baseball's history includes women. Formal women's teams began in the 1870s at colleges such as Vassar and Smith. Starting in 1943 and throughout World War II, the All American Girls Professional Baseball League captured fan interest for 12 years.

Baseball also was a part of the United States' segregated past. Once, few African Americans were permitted to play with white players. Black players played in their own leagues, called the Negro Leagues. There were many great black players, such as Josh Gibson, Satchel Paige, and Rube Foster.

In 1947, Jackie Robinson became the first black man to play in the major leagues. Although most of his

Babe Ruth held the major league record for home runs in a career (714) from 1935 . . .

. . . until Hank Aaron hit his 715th home run in 1974. Aaron retired in 1976 with 755 homers.

The Colorado Silver Bullets, a minor league team made up entirely of women, began playing other minor league teams in 1994.

teammates on the Brooklyn Dodgers supported him, Robinson endured many ugly taunts and threats. He was the National League Rookie of the Year in 1947 and the National League's Most Valuable Player in 1949. He led the way into the major leagues for thousands of black players.

Baseball has flourished outside of the United States in Canada, the Dominican Republic, Cuba, Japan, Mexico, Puerto Rico, and Nicaragua.

If you want to provoke an interesting conversation, ask someone what his or her favorite baseball memory is. Perhaps it was watching Don Larson's perfect game in the 1956 World Series. Or Joe Carter's dramatic home run in the 1993 Series. Maybe your friend's favorite memory is when he struck out five batters in a Little League game, or when she first completed a double play. What's your favorite baseball memory?

Roberto Alomar helped the Toronto Blue Jays win the World Series in 1992 and 1993.

Ty Cobb, a star in organized baseball's early days, developed nine different ways to slide into base.

Chapter 2

BASICS

To play baseball, you will need a bat, a ball, and a glove.

In baseball's earliest days, the baseballs themselves were homemade items made from twisted yarn covered by calfskin. Modern baseballs are manufactured by machines.

A baseball is 9 to 9¼ inches around and weighs 5 to 5¼ ounces. The white cowhide (or synthetic leather) cover is stitched with heavy red thread. Underneath the covering is a small cork center surrounded by two layers of rubber and three layers of yarn.

A bat is a long, smooth piece of wood—usually ash—or aluminum. The first baseball bats might have been made from an old wagon wheel spoke. Aluminum bats are used in youth, high school, and college play because they don't break, but they are illegal in professional baseball. A bat can't be longer than 42 inches and it can't be wider than 2¼ inches at its widest point. The handle of an aluminum bat is covered with a rubber or leather grip and ends in a

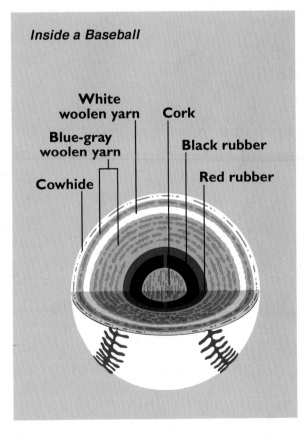

Inside a Baseball

White woolen yarn

Blue-gray woolen yarn

Cowhide

Cork

Black rubber

Red rubber

knob. The portion of the bat that hits the ball is called the barrel.

Choose a light bat that you can swing easily. Most hitters struggle with a bat that is too heavy because they think the heavier the bat, the more power it will generate. But the lighter your bat is, the quicker your swing will be. The quicker your swing, the harder you will hit the ball.

Stretch out your weaker arm at shoulder height. If you can hold the bat level without struggling, it is the correct weight for you. The correct bat length is whatever feels the best when swinging, but the bat should be no more than 3 to 8 inches longer than the number of ounces it weighs. Here are some suggestions:

- ages up to 8 years: 15 to 21 ounces
- 9 to 12 years: 21 to 25 ounces
- up to 18 years: 25 to 32 ounces

You will need a glove that fits the position you most often play. If you are an infielder, choose a small glove so that you can get the ball out of your glove quickly. A pitcher, outfielder, or first baseman needs a larger glove to help scoop up the ball. A catcher needs a special mitt with a padded palm.

When buying a glove, don't just buy the biggest glove or one autographed by your favorite player. Huge gloves can lead to bad habits, like not using your hands properly or not using both hands to make a catch.

A baseball player wears a hard plastic cap when batting. This batting helmet protects the batter from a

Baseball Gloves

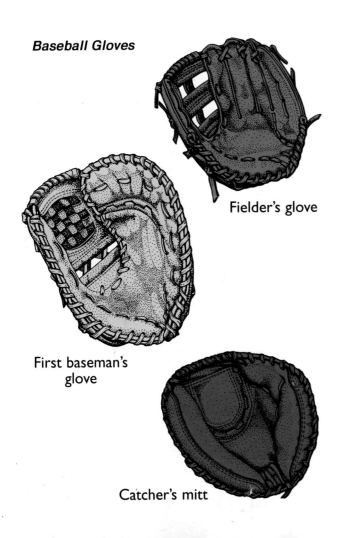

Fielder's glove

First baseman's glove

Catcher's mitt

pitched ball while batting and a thrown ball while running the bases. Batting helmets are required in all leagues.

Many baseball players also wear spiked shoes, called cleats, to improve their running. Some also wear a tight-fitting glove, called a batting glove, when they are batting. A batting glove helps these players grip the bat better.

And nearly every baseball player—and even many people who don't play baseball—wears a baseball cap. The wide brim of the cap helps to keep the sun out of a player's eyes.

THE FIELD

A baseball field has an infield, an outfield, and foul territory. The infield is a square area, usually dirt, with a base at each corner. Because the infield looks diamond-shaped from behind home plate, baseball fields are called diamonds.

The outfield is the grassy section between the infield and the fence that borders the field. The size of the outfield varies from field to field.

The infield and outfield are fair territory, which is where the game is played. Foul territory is the area outside the infield and outside the foul lines of the outfield. The foul lines are marked with white chalk. One line extends from each side of home plate to the fence.

The pitcher throws the ball from the pitcher's mound, which is 60 feet, 6 inches from home plate. The mound is 18 feet wide and 10 inches high in the center. In the center is a piece of white rubber, 24 inches long and 6 inches wide, known as the rubber. The pitcher's foot must be touching the rubber when he or she releases a pitch.

Outfield

Foul line

Foul territory

Second base

90' (60')

Infield

Third base

Pitcher's mound

Pitching rubber

60' 6" (46')

Home plate

First, second, and third bases are white canvas bags filled with sand. The bases are 15 inches square and 5 inches thick. Each base is 90 feet from the next one.

Home plate is a five-sided piece of white rubber. The part of home plate that is nearest the infield is 17 inches wide. Home plate narrows to a point on the side farthest from the infield. The ball is pitched over home plate, and batters stand beside it when taking their swings at the ball. A rectangle, 6 feet by 4 feet, is marked with chalk on each side of home plate. These areas are called the **batter's box.** A batter must be standing in either the left-side or right-side batter's box when the pitch is thrown.

The measurements for Little League play are shown in parentheses ( ).

90' (60')

Foul line

Foul territory

First base

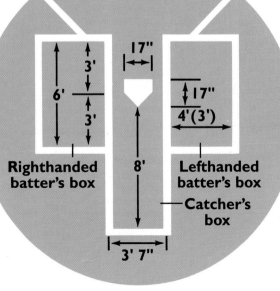

Home Plate Area

Righthanded batter's box

Lefthanded batter's box

Catcher's box

17"

3'

6'

3'

17"

4' (3')

8'

3' 7"

THE RULES

A game begins when the pitcher puts his or her foot on the rubber of the pitcher's mound. Then the pitcher throws the ball to the catcher, who crouches behind home plate. The pitcher tries to pitch so that the ball crosses the plate within the **strike zone,** an imaginary rectangle from the batter's armpits to knees that is the width of home plate.

A **strike** is called when the batter either swings at the ball and misses or doesn't swing at a pitch that the umpire says was in the strike zone. When three strikes have been called, that batter has made an **out,** called a **strikeout.**

A **ball** is called when the batter doesn't swing at a pitch and the umpire rules that the ball was outside of the strike zone. If four balls are called, the batter is given a **base on balls,** or walk, which means he or she goes to first base.

When the batter hits the ball in fair territory, the game explodes into action. The batter's **hit** sends fielders sprinting all over the field. If the hit ball is caught in the air, the batter is out. But if the ball isn't caught before it hits the ground, the hitter becomes a baserunner. A baserunner's goal is to touch all the bases. Safely reaching home plate records one run for the team at bat. Of course, the team in

the field tries to prevent baserunners from reaching base and scoring runs.

Once a baserunner has reached a base, he or she is safe and can't be tagged out while still touching the base. The runner can remain on a base until the next batter gets a hit. Once the ball is in play again, the baserunner can continue the challenge of advancing to the next base.

A baserunner is tagged out if he or she isn't on a base and is touched by a fielder who is holding the ball. If a fielder touches a base while holding the ball before the baserunner touches the base, the runner is out if all the bases behind him or her are occupied. This is a **forceout**. The runner can also be forced out at first base.

If a batter gets to first base safely, that batter has hit a single. If the batter gets to second base, the hit is a double. If the batter reaches third base, the hit is a triple. If the batter reaches home plate on the hit, the batter has hit a **home run.**

If a player hits the ball and a fielder makes a mistake—throws the ball over the first baseman's head, for example—the batter reaches base on an **error.** If a batter hits the ball but reaches first base safely only because the fielders decided to force out a baserunner instead of making the play on the batter, the play is called a **fielder's choice.** If the fielding team puts out two baserunners during one play, the fielders have made a **double play.** Often, a double play is made when a baserunner is on first base and the batter hits the ball to the infield. The fielders can force out the runner at second base and still get the ball to first base before the batter gets there.

Over the past 150 years, baseball has developed some complicated rules to make the game fair. One such rule is the infield fly rule. The rule applies when there are no outs or one out and at least two runners on base who could be forced out. If the batter hits a **popfly** that could be caught by an infielder, the umpire yells "Infield fly. The batter's out!" This prevents a fielder from intentionally dropping the ball in order to make a double play. A baserunner may advance "at his or her own risk" if the ball is dropped.

A baseball game is usually six, seven, or nine innings, depending on the level of play. The visiting team bats first in the game, and each team has one turn at bat with three outs per inning. The exception to this rule is in the last inning, when the home team doesn't bat if it is ahead.

When a team is batting, the players on that team bat in an assigned order, called the **lineup.** The manager decides the batting order. The player who is batting is "up." The next player to bat is "on deck," and the player following him or her is "in the hole." Coaches near first base and third base help the baserunners decide when to run.

An umpire calls balls and strikes from behind home plate. The umpire also makes sure the other rules of the game are followed. If there are two or more umpires, the additional umpires are stationed around the bases to rule on whether baserunners are safe or out. If there is only one umpire, he or she must run from behind the plate out into the infield to make base calls.

FIELDING

Baseball is a simple game. There are only four maneuvers a baseball player must be able to do: field the ball, throw the ball, hit the ball, and run. But baseball isn't an easy game. It will take time and effort to learn how to handle the ball, throw it accurately, hit it, and run efficiently.

Each team uses nine fielders when it isn't batting. Each fielder has an area of the field to cover. The pitcher covers the area near the mound. The catcher covers home. The first baseman, second baseman, and third baseman all play near their bases. The shortstop plays between second and third bases. These four players are infielders. The three outfielders are spread across the outfield.

To become a good fielder, learn to catch without a glove. Practice using "soft hands." Soft hands cradle the ball gently rather than let the ball slap stiffly against them. Try to catch the ball so that very little sound is heard as it hits your hands. Pretend your hands are glass—if the ball hits your hands too hard, your hands will shatter.

Ken Griffey Jr. began his major league career in the Seattle Mariners' outfield. He was the first American League outfielder to win five straight Gold Gloves.

Dave and Andy are using their bare hands to catch a tennis ball. First, Andy runs five steps away from his coach, who lobs the ball ahead of Andy. Andy looks over his shoulder, finds the ball, and runs to catch it. The coach alternates his throws, first to the left, then to the right.

After both players have caught 10 balls, they use their gloves and a baseball. Dave runs 10 steps before looking over his shoulder. Dave and Andy don't reach out with the glove until the last instant before catching the ball. Running with your glove hand extended slows you down and prevents you from making a catch.

FIELDING GROUND BALLS

Matt and Katy are fielding **ground balls.** Because the grass and dirt of the infield is uneven, fielding ground balls takes patience and practice.

As he waits for the batter to hit the ball, Matt's back is bent slightly forward and his hands rest comfortably on his bent knees. He has spread his legs wider than his shoulders to get as low as possible. This gives Matt better balance and enables him to get closer to the ground. He keeps his balance by having his weight on the balls of his feet.

Matt throws with his right hand, so his right foot is slightly behind his left. With his throwing-side foot back, he is able to throw quicker.

Matt has his glove fully open and on the ground. Most errors are caused by balls going under the glove, not over it, so keep your glove touching the ground. Extend your arm in front of you so that you can see the ball go into the glove.

Matt's right hand is above the glove. With his glove extended forward, not downward, it can't tangle up Matt's feet. With Matt's hands extended, he can better react to bad hops. His hands can cushion the ball, like shock absorbers. Then he can smoothly bring the ball to the throwing position.

Keep your feet moving when you are fielding a ground ball. Here, Katy is running quickly to the ball. By charging the ball, she reaches it quicker and her throw is shorter. Remember, the longer the fielder takes to catch and throw the ball, the more time the baserunner has.

When Katy reaches the ball, she slows and spreads her legs to get as low to the ground as she can. Katy uses both hands to field the

grounder. This way, the ball is less likely to pop out of her glove. She watches the ball go into her glove.

Katy's top hand acts like a garbage can cover. As the ball enters her glove, her throwing hand covers the ball. Using both hands also means Katy will be able to throw the ball quicker since her throwing hand is already touching the ball.

When you field a ground ball, use both hands and try to create a fluid motion instead of a two-step action. Practice doing this in slow motion without a ball until you can do it smoothly with no wasted motion.

FIELDING FLY BALLS AND POPUPS

When catching a **fly ball** or popup, remember to use soft hands. In the photos on this page, Missy is catching a fly ball above her waist, so her gloved fingers are pointed up. When possible, try to catch the ball above your head. That way, your glove can serve as a shield to keep the sun out of your eyes, and you can watch the ball more easily. If you fumble the ball, you have a second try at catching it before it hits the ground.

Trying to catch a ball below your waist with your fingers pointing up is awkward. If you must catch a fly ball below your waist, have your glove pointing down. In the photograph above, Ben is catching a fly ball below his waist. His gloved fingers are pointed down.

When you must run to catch a fly ball, run on the balls of your feet, not your heels. Running on your heels causes your body to bounce. Running on the balls of your feet cushions your body, and helps keep your vision steady. That way, you can watch the ball until it lands in your glove.

Chapter 4

THROWING

After fielding the ball, you must make a good throw to complete the play. Be sure your shoulders are level and that your front shoulder points directly toward your target. Step directly toward the target with your lead foot.

A good throw begins with the proper grip. Katy splits her index and middle finger ½ to 1 inch across the ball's big seams. The pads directly below these fingertips grip the ball loosely. (If your hand is smaller than Katy's, grip the ball with three fingers.)

Katy's thumb is placed directly underneath and toward the middle of the baseball. The ball rests on the side of the thumb, not the pad of the thumb tip. There is about a half-inch between Katy's palm and the ball.

Hold the ball loosely in your hand for maximum power. About 15 percent of your throwing power comes from snapping your wrist during the throwing motion. Holding the ball too tightly locks your wrist.

33

Katy's weight is on the ball of her back foot, which is at a 90-degree angle to her target. Katy's back leg is bent as if she were preparing to take a jump shot in basketball. Katy will drive forward off of her back leg toward the target.

Katy's shoulders are level, not sloped toward the sky or the ground. Your front shoulder aims the ball. If your shoulders slope upward, your throw will be a high one. If your shoulders aim to the right or left of the target, the ball will go in that direction.

Katy's glove is at shoulder level, about 12 inches out from her shoulder. Her elbow is down and her wrist is bent.

After you grip the ball, you must cock your arm for the throw. Katy's arm is behind her. Her palm is down and her elbow is level or slightly above her shoulder. The farther Katy can comfortably extend her arm backward without her elbow locking, the more power she will generate. This is called the eagle position. Think of extending your arm back with the wingspan of an eagle.

Keep the ball just above head height when in this position. If your elbow drops and the ball is below head height, you will push the ball and your throw will be high.

TAKE CARE OF YOUR ARM

A strong arm takes years to develop. If your arm is injured, your baseball career can be crippled. So take care of your arm! In cool weather, wear a T-shirt, a nylon jacket, and a sweatshirt as minimum protection. You can always take off a layer if you get too hot.

Before throwing, warm up your muscles by jogging. Then stretch by doing toe touches and arm circles. Start to throw by lobbing the ball half the distance from the plate to the mound. Gradually increase the distance until you're throwing from the plate to second base. Easy throwing for five minutes will get you ready.

Don't throw hard or for a long time, especially early in the season. Stop throwing any time your shoulder, elbow, or wrist starts to hurt.

From this cocking position, Katy shifts most of her weight to her back leg. She keeps her shoulders level. Katy's palm has rotated from facing the ground to facing the sky, and her wrist is cocked back.

She steps forward 6 to 12 inches directly toward her target with her front foot, landing on the ball of that foot. This allows a complete follow-through. As she pushes off her back leg and steps toward the target, Katy's front hip rotates so her knee and foot point to the target.

As her front foot hits the ground, her arm thrusts forward. Katy's elbow, level or slightly above her shoulder, leads the thrust as her weight shifts forward, aided by her front side rotating down toward the front hip. Katy whips the ball ahead of her elbow, snapping her wrist, and releases the ball when her arm is fully extended.

For an outfield throw, Matt uses a technique called the *crow hop*. He hops on his back foot with his instep pointing to the target and releases the ball as he steps directly toward the target with his front foot.

Katy's throwing hand finishes on the outside of her forward knee. Her back is bent, and her back leg swings forward so that her back foot ends up slightly ahead of her front foot.

THROWING PRACTICE

Practice your throwing motion 25 times a day in slow motion, and you will have a smooth, powerful, and balanced throw. While you practice, be aware of using all your muscles in your feet, legs, sides, back, shoulders, arm, and wrist.

Throw as much as you can. Play catch with friends anywhere and as often as possible. Throwing against a wall also helps. Gradually increase the number and the distance of your throws. If you only throw 90 feet, your arm will never get stronger.

Dave and Andy are making high, lazy, long throws, not hard line drives. This strengthens their arms without injuring them. Throw as much and as often as your arm permits. But remember, stop throwing if you feel sore. You only have one good throwing arm. Take care of it!

Chapter 5

HITTING

Hitting is the most challenging part of baseball—and the most fun. Don't expect a hit every time. View each **at bat** as a challenge. If you strike out, don't get discouraged. Concentrate on getting a hit the next time. A hitter is considered successful if he or she gets a hit 3 out of every 10 at bats. Successful players learn from their mistakes and tell themselves to improve next time.

Hitting seems very complex but there is only one goal: hit the ball squarely with as quick a swing as possible. Once you have mastered this, you will have a good swing. Then when you enter the batter's box, you will have only two things to think about: selecting a good pitch to hit and hitting a **line drive** to centerfield.

A good swing begins with the correct grip. Dave holds the bat just above the pads below his fingertips with the bottom three fingers of each hand relaxed. Notice how his finger knuckles (those you use when knocking on a door), not his hand knuckles, line up.

Dave holds the bat firmly, as he would hold a hammer, but not too tightly. Tension is a hitter's enemy. Squeezing the bat too hard slows down your swing and decreases your control.

SWINGING

Practice swinging the bat at imaginary baseballs. (But be sure real lamps aren't nearby!) Get the feel of throwing the barrel quickly and precisely through the ball.

Good hitting begins with a solid base. Dave's feet are slightly wider than his shoulders. His weight is on the balls of his feet. He has bent both knees slightly, unlocking his legs' power, so that if he looks down he sees his knees but not his feet.

Dave rests the bat on his shoulder at a 45-degree angle. His top hand is near the top of his rear shoulder. The bat's knob is facing down at his back toe, not toward the catcher. If the knob is facing the catcher, Dave's bat would have a longer path to the ball.

When the pitcher begins the windup, Dave lifts the bat off his shoulder, keeping it at a 45-degree angle. His top hand is even with the top of his back shoulder.

Dave keeps his hands 3 to 5 inches from his body. You have more strength when your hands are close to your body. But don't bring your hands too close to your body, or you will not be able to swing freely.

Dave's eyes, shoulders, and elbows are level to ensure good vision and a level swing. If one elbow or one shoulder was higher than the other, Dave's swing would probably be either an uppercut or a downward chop.

His front elbow is relaxed. It points down and is toward the front of his body, but not past his belly button. If Dave's front elbow was back too far,

his arms would be locked in a more rigid position. That would slow down his swing and make an inside pitch harder for him to hit.

Dave's head is turned so both of his eyes are looking directly at the pitcher. His chin is near his front shoulder. Be sure to turn your head far enough so that your eyes are not blocked by your nose or the bridge of your glasses.

To begin the swing, Ben cocks his lower body and hands. When you do this, imagine that your pants have a back pocket on the leg closest to the pitcher. When the pitcher raises his or her leg to pitch, turn your lower body one inch so that the pocket points toward the pitcher. This will cock the front hip and put your weight properly over the back foot.

At the same time Ben cocks his hips, he moves his hands back one or two inches. Imagine a string connecting the hands and hips. As your hip pocket cocks one inch, your hands cock back at the same time.

Keep the bat as still as possible when cocking. Starting the bat from the same position each time results in a consistent swing.

Next, Ben takes a short, two-inch stride forward with his front foot. When striding, your weight will shift from your back leg to your front leg. Your weight should be evenly balanced on both legs after the stride.

As the pitch is released, Ben strides forward by lifting his knee about an inch so the front foot is raised onto its ball and the heel is slightly raised. Stride directly toward the pitcher. A short, balanced stride is key to successful hitting.

Ben lands on the ball of his front foot and, as his swing continues, he shifts his weight to his heel. When striding, imagine that you are stepping onto a thin piece of ice. Stepping too hard would send you crashing into the water.

When the bat hits the ball, Ben is looking down his arms and the barrel of the bat. His eyes are focused on the ball. His chin is near his back shoulder and his upper body and chest are balanced, not leaning over the plate. Ben's back elbow is close to his body but his arms are almost fully extended.

Ben's hips have rotated to release his lower body's power, like a giant spring uncoiling. His back foot has pivoted 90 degrees so his toe points toward the pitcher. This motion is like squishing a bug. The player who doesn't squish the bug isn't releasing all of his or her power.

The point at which the bat contacts the ball is slightly ahead of Ben's body, where his bat speed is the fastest. Ben's bottom hand and left elbow pull down and directly toward the pitcher while his top hand throws the barrel of the bat toward and through the ball. Ben's top arm extends at contact.

By thrusting his hands toward the pitcher and throwing the barrel ahead of his hands and through the ball, Ben has a quick, compact swing. When you are swinging, keep your hands close to your body and whip the barrel through the ball.

As Ben follows through, he keeps his head still and his eyes focused on the point of contact. Train your head and eyes to stay down and focused on the contact point even after you have hit the ball. Your hands should finish up near your front shoulder.

Release your top hand after contact if that's comfortable for you. Some great hitters have been successful, however, keeping both hands on the bat even after contacting the ball. The key to success is doing what works best for you.

PRACTICE = PERFECTION

After you have learned the fundamentals of hitting, there is only one way for you to become a better hitter. You must practice, and practice correctly. Practice doesn't necessarily make perfect, practice makes permanent. So with every swing, practice perfectly so perfection becomes permanent.

Start with this practice routine:

1. Each day choose one or two parts of the swing to improve.

2. Swing 25 times in slow motion.

3. Then take 25 good swings, thinking about the part of the swing you're working on. A good practice swing is not just waving a bat in the air. Imagine yourself in a real game. Visualize yourself hitting pitches in all parts of the strike zone. Feel confident. Feel relaxed.

4. Next, hit 25 balls off of a tee. You can use whiffle balls or tennis balls.

THE MENTAL GAME

Develop a positive attitude. Practice daily, by yourself and with friends, and you will improve. Set realistic goals. Try to get on base once a game with a walk, error, or hit. Once you reach this goal, every other time you get on base is a bonus.

While you are sitting in the dugout during a game, study the other team's pitcher. Try to learn that pitcher's patterns. Are this pitcher's pitches usually high or low? What pitches does this pitcher throw when starting a batter, when ahead in the count, and when behind in the count?

Have a plan at the plate. Be selective, but be aggressive. Attack every good pitch. Don't swing at pitches you don't like. Don't worry about your mechanics at the plate.

Focus on the pitcher's release point and try to see the seams of the ball spin. Try to see the ball hit your bat, and practice keeping your head down at the contact point until your follow-through is completed.

Study the pitcher's grip, the release point, and the spin of the ball to distinguish a **fastball,** a **change-up,** or a **curveball.** If the pitcher falls behind

in the count by throwing balls, you can be choosy. Before you have a strike against you, look for the pitch that you can hit best. Your best pitch may be high or low, to the inside or to the outside part of the plate. Always look for a fastball toward the middle of the plate when you have an advantage in the count.

With one strike, you can't be as picky. Look for a pitch you can drive, even if it's not in your favorite spot. With two strikes, focus on hitting the ball somewhere. Be aggressive—don't let the umpire's call determine your success.

To raise your **batting average,** focus on hitting a line drive over the pitcher's head on every pitch. Why? Hitting up the middle gives you more chances to find an open spot. If your timing is correct, the ball will be a single up the middle. If your swing is just a little early or late, the single could become an extra-base hit to leftfield or rightfield.

Also, the middle is the most open area of the field. The shortstop and second baseman are on either side of second base. The pitcher is often off balance after releasing the ball. A hard-hit ball up the middle gives the pitcher and infielders little time to react and field the ball cleanly.

WHOLE-BODY HITTING

Use all your muscles when hitting. Your legs, hips, and back muscles are much stronger than just your arms and hands. Get on your knees and try to swing. Notice how little power is generated by the arms alone. Use your entire body when hitting.

To *pull* the ball means to hit it to leftfield if you are a righthanded hitter, or rightfield if you are lefthanded. To pull the ball, Ben hits it farther in front of his body. To hit to centerfield, Ben hits the ball slightly in front of his body with the barrel slightly ahead of his wrists. To hit the ball to the opposite field (rightfield for a righthander), Ben hits the ball when it is even or slightly behind his body.

Bunting—softly tapping a pitch so that it drops on the infield grass—can cause more confusion than any other play in baseball. Learning to bunt also develops your timing and helps you see the ball better. With practice, anyone can become an excellent bunter. The following steps explain a **sacrifice** bunt where the main goal is to advance a runner. However, a good bunt often gets you on base.

Bunting begins with a good soft grip. Take your back hand and make an imaginary squirt gun with your thumb extended upward and your index finger pointed outward, as Katy illustrates. Pull your index finger as if you were pulling the trigger so your finger is curled inward. You have made a V with the base of the thumb and the fleshy area that extends to the fingers. The bat should rest loosely in the V. Your fingers and thumb are protected behind the surface of the bat, not wrapped around it.

Loosely grip the handle of the bat with your other hand's fingers wrapped around the handle. This hand should be 12 to 18 inches from the knob. The bat's barrel should slant upward and be close to eye level. Keep the bat higher than the ball to avoid popping up. Move forward in the batter's box so the bat is in fair territory. This increases your chances of a fair, not foul, bunt. A foul bunt is a strike.

There are two stances for bunting: the pivot and the square-off. In both stances, the batter's knees are bent so that his or her strike zone is lower.

The pivot stance is the easiest method. The hitter stands a little closer to the plate and pivots on the balls of his or her feet until his or her hips face the pitcher.

In the square-off stance, the batter steps away from the plate with his or her front foot until it is parallel with his or her back foot and with the side of the batter's box. Both hips face the pitcher and the feet are spread wider than shoulder-width apart.

Ben holds the bat's barrel at the top of the strike zone and over the entire width of the plate. He moves his bat in just one direction—down. He brings the bat to the ball by bending his knees and lowering his body, not his hands. He lets the ball come to the bat. Think of "catching" the ball with the bat.

To practice bunting, pick out a couple of letters from the brand name on your bat, 3 or 4 inches from the end of the bat. Try to see the ball hit those letters on your bat when you bunt.

Bunting is fun to practice. Have a friend stand 10 to 20 feet away from you. Put a target where each baseline would be. Have your friend toss you a soft pitch and try to bunt it to one of the targets. Switch positions after every 10 pitches.

BASERUNNING

Aggressive baserunning changes a predictable game into a game of chance and daring. To be a good baserunner, you must first be a good runner. Start with a relaxed body. Tight muscles will reduce your speed. Keep your feet pointed straight ahead and explode off the balls of your feet with your knees pumping almost to your waist and your heels kicking back to your buttocks. Pump your arms along the sides of your body, not across it. Your hands should pump to eye level.

When you have mastered good running form, concentrate on these two principles of baserunning: always run as fast as you can and be as aggressive as possible.

When you run at top speed, you force the fielders to make their play cleanly and without delay. Fielders are more apt to make a mistake if they are worrying about you hustling down to first. If the fielders do make a mistake or hesitate, be ready to take an extra base.

Baserunning begins at home plate. After Dave hits the ball, he drops his bat after following through. He sprints down the first baseline until he gets halfway to first base. Then he makes sure he is running in foul territory (to the right of the line). If a fielder's throw hits Dave while he is in fair territory, the umpire will call him out for interference.

Dave runs two or three steps past first base before slowing down, just in case he can take advantage of a misplay and go to second base. If Dave turns toward second base, the fielders may try to tag him out even

though he has already touched first base. But if Dave turns toward foul territory to return to first base, he's entitled to safely return to the base.

If Dave's hit reaches the outfield, his goal is second base. He sprints to first base but rounds the base by veering to his right 4 to 6 feet when

he is two-thirds of the way there. He touches first base with his right foot and pushes off toward second.

Round the bag with as tight a turn as you can so that your first step after touching first takes you directly toward second. Make tight turns when running all the bases.

An aggressive lead gives a baserunner the best possible chance of advancing to the next base, either on a hit or a **stolen base.** When leading off, always watch the pitcher, not your feet. You want to be as far off the base as possible, usually 10 to 15 feet, without getting put out.

Don't jump off the base when leading off. Ben has his right toe on the corner of first base and is facing second base. He takes a 2-foot step with his left foot and then a 2-foot step with his right foot. Ben turns and faces home plate before taking two 2½-foot shuffle steps toward second base. Have your weight on the balls of your feet and keep your body fairly upright and relaxed.

Ben's first movement to the next base is to throw his left arm across his body as he pivots on his right foot. Then he uses good running form.

Another good technique is the walking lead. Walk toward the next base as the pitcher releases the ball. As the ball crosses home plate, stop but lean toward the next base. Then, if the pitch gets past the catcher or is hit, you have a head start.

Ben, the baserunner, is as far from second base as is the closest fielder—in this case, Dave, the second baseman.

When you are on second base, you can lead off as far as the shortstop and second baseman are from the bag. For example, the closest fielder, Dave, is 15 feet from the bag, so Ben is leading off about 15 feet. Try to lead off 5 feet behind a straight line from second base to third base. This helps you watch the second baseman and shortstop. Also, you are in position to round third base and sprint for home.

A good trick is to take an extra-long lead and dare the catcher to pick you off of second base. As the catcher releases the ball, sprint to third. You will be on third before the fielder can catch the ball and throw to third.

When you're on second base, don't run when a ball is hit to your right unless there's a runner on first or you are positive that the ball will reach the outfield. But, if the ball is hit to your left, sprint for third. The fielder will have to field the ball and throw across the infield.

When leading off third base, as Missy is, stand 2 feet in foul territory and as far from third base as the third baseman is.

As the pitch is released, Missy takes two steps toward home plate and leans forward. She's ready to sprint home if the ball gets past the catcher or if the batter gets a hit.

To steal a base, a baserunner must watch the pitcher. If you want to see a pitcher's **pickoff move,** just take a slightly longer lead to draw a throw. Be ready to rush back to the base on the pitcher's first move. Once you know the pitcher's move, you're better prepared to steal.

When a righthanded pitcher raises his or her front foot in order to throw a pitch, the baserunner can start for the next base. A lefthander could step toward first base. If the pitcher steps off the rubber with his or her back foot, the pitcher cannot throw a pitch and is likely to throw to a base.

Sooner or later, you will need to **slide.** Sliding is helpful when you're trying to avoid being tagged, running into a fielder, or overrunning a base. Wear long, heavy pants when you're learning to slide, and practice in stocking feet on the grass.

On this page, Dave starts his slide when he's about 10 feet from the base. He lifts both feet from the ground at the same time. Glide into the slide. Dave extends his right leg to the base and bends his left leg. He turns his left foot out to the side so his spikes don't catch in the dirt.

Dave raises his arms above and behind his head. He touches the base with his left foot. Dave pushes off with his right foot to boost himself upright. Then he can quickly go on to third base if the ball was overthrown on the play.

Chapter 7

ON THE FIELD

Baseball's nine positions each require special physical and mental skills, but catching, throwing, and running fundamentals are used at all the positions. You also need concentration, good work habits, judgment, and confidence to be successful.

Work on developing skills, but have fun. You will improve. After you have practiced the fundamentals, you'll want to use those skills in a game.

College coach Lefty Cyson once said, "You can't play well unless you're relaxed. So relax! You can't be relaxed unless you're having fun. So go out and have fun!" Don't let anyone—fans, parents, coaches, teammates, or opponents—wreck your fun.

PITCHER

Good pitching gives your team the chance to win every game. Besides a strong and accurate throwing arm, confidence is the most important ingredient in a pitcher.

As a pitcher, you will have discouraging days. Sometimes you will walk many batters. You may be called for a **balk.** Great pitches may be called balls by umpires or turned into game-winning hits by opponents.

Remember—the only real pressure you have is the pressure you put on yourself. Concentrate on hitting the catcher's glove. Don't listen to anyone's distracting voice. Have confidence that with hard work you will be successful. See each pitching appearance as a challenge and an opportunity to improve.

To become a good pitcher, there are four basic body positions to learn. All the motions require balance. Practice these motions in front of a mirror.

Jay will demonstrate these positions. He's lefthanded. If you're not, just pretend you are looking in a mirror and use the opposite hand or foot that Jay is using.

Jay starts with his feet shoulder-width apart. His front foot is 6 inches toward the first baseline. He keeps the ball hidden in his glove. The glove is held at chest level.

Jay lifts his front knee above his waist so that his glove is a few inches above his knee. His weight is on the ball of his back foot. His knee is bent, as if he were going to jump. Think of your knee and its foot as a puppet's.

is bent slightly. This coiling of his arm creates more power.

Jay's upper body can supply him with extra power. Think about Dracula raising his cape to hide his fangs. Jay uses that motion with his glove arm as his other arm is lifting the ball. Jay lifts the glove about 10 inches away from his front shoulder. His elbow is down and his glove wrist is bent loosely.

When you lift your knee, keep your foot directly underneath it. When your foot is directly below your knee, your body is balanced. Balance is the key concept. Being balanced gives your body its maximum power.

After Jay brings his glove above his knee, he takes the ball out of the glove into the eagle position. In this position, his palm is facing down, his hand is above head height and his elbow is above his shoulder.

When Jay whips the ball forward and downward from this position, gravity helps accelerate the ball. Jay reaches back comfortably, his elbow

Jay is poised to throw. He pulls his front elbow down toward his hip as he cocks his throwing wrist so that the fingers are on top of the ball and his palm is facing upward.

As he pulls down his front elbow, Jay steps forward on his front leg. He lands on the ball of his front foot. His front foot points directly toward home plate.

As Jay's back leg pushes forward, the front of his body pulls his arm forward. His wrist whips the ball directly toward the catcher's mitt. He releases the ball when it is 2 to 3 feet in front of his body, at about the level of his hat. The toe of his front foot points directly toward the catcher's mitt.

Jay continues to push off his back leg. As his front side pulls him forward and down, he shifts his weight so that he finishes with the back foot even with or slightly ahead of the front foot. Meanwhile, his throwing arm continues to its full extension. His throwing hand finishes near his opposite knee. After completing his follow-through, Jay gets into a ready position so that he can field any ball hit his way.

THROWING ACROSS YOUR BODY

Throwing across your body can hurt your throwing shoulder. If your front foot steps across your body, it prevents your hips and front side from rotating fully.

To avoid throwing across your body, make a line in the dirt or tape a straight line on the floor directly toward your target. Then check where your foot lands. It should land on the line or tape to ensure the correct, direct step to the target. This simple test can help keep your arm strong and healthy.

CATCHER

A catcher must be tough, alert, have a strong arm, and a good understanding of baseball. A catcher also must not mind being hit by the ball or by incoming baserunners.

A catcher often tells the pitcher what pitch to throw and where, using hand signals. To do this, Andy squats with his buttocks on his heels. His back is straight, and his glove rests on his left knee to block the third base coach's view. Andy's right hand is between his legs. Using his fingers, he signals to the pitcher which pitch to throw.

When there is a runner on base, the catcher must be able to quickly throw the ball after a pitch. Andy spreads his legs a little wider and extends his glove toward the pitcher. His throwing hand is behind his back or the glove. After catching the ball, Andy brings it back to the eagle position as if drawing back a spear. At the same time, he steps directly toward the target.

Catchers must also block balls that are thrown in the dirt. To do this, Andy falls to his knees with his glove on the ground, blocking the space between his knees. He hunches forward with his shoulders and tucks his chin.

FIRST BASE

A first baseman must be able to catch all types of throws and cover the bag. This player doesn't have to be fast or have great range, but being tall is helpful when receiving a high throw from a fielder.

To catch any throw, the first baseman must sprint to the bag as soon as the hitter makes contact. The first baseman places a foot on the front of the bag and faces the fielder who is making the play. The first baseman keeps his or her foot on the bag and stretches as far as possible to receive the ball as quickly as possible.

Perhaps the most difficult play for a first baseman is catching a throw in the dirt. Be sure your glove is on the ground and extended outward so your elbow is almost straight. Pretend that your glove is made of glass. If the ball hits it too hard, the glove will break. Keep your body loose and "give" with the ball to soften the ball's impact. Watch the ball go into your glove.

SECOND BASE

A second baseman needs to have quick feet, good hands, and a quick release. Two of the most important plays a second baseman must make are tagging the runner and turning a double play. To tag a baserunner, the second baseman must sprint to the bag and straddle the bag. After you catch the ball, sweep your glove down and tag the bag. This way, the runner tags himself or herself out trying to touch the base. If you reach out for the runner, he or she may slide underneath or around your tag. Apply the tag with both hands.

The footwork for turning a double play is perhaps the most graceful movement in baseball. If the ball is hit to the third-base side of second base, the second baseman sprints to the bag and straddles it to receive the throw. Once the second baseman has the ball, that player must square his or her shoulders and face directly toward first while throwing the ball to the first baseman.

If the ball is hit to the first-base side of second, the second baseman fields the ball and the shortstop covers second base.

WALL BALL

Here's how to practice your fielding and throwing form. Find a flat, smooth surface leading up to a wall, sturdy garage door, or steps. Practice throwing a rubber ball against this surface. When working out against the wall, remember to get low by spreading your feet wider than your shoulders. Also, keep your throwing-side foot slightly behind your other foot.

SHORTSTOP

A shortstop needs quickness, range, confidence, good hands, and a strong, accurate throwing arm. A shortstop must field the ball, back up other fielders, and direct outfielders on where to throw the ball. The shortstop has so much ground to cover that he or she must anticipate plays.

THIRD BASE

The third baseman needs good hands and a strong arm. A common play for a third baseman is to field a bunt down the third baseline. The third baseman must charge the ball, field it, and throw it accurately.

The third baseman must run full-speed to the ball. When he or she reaches it, the third baseman crou-ches down to field the ball. If the ball is not moving, the third baseman can pick it up with his or her bare hand. If the ball is moving, the third baseman should catch it with the glove and both hands. Catch the ball with the left foot forward. Then, still crouched, step forward on the right foot and throw.

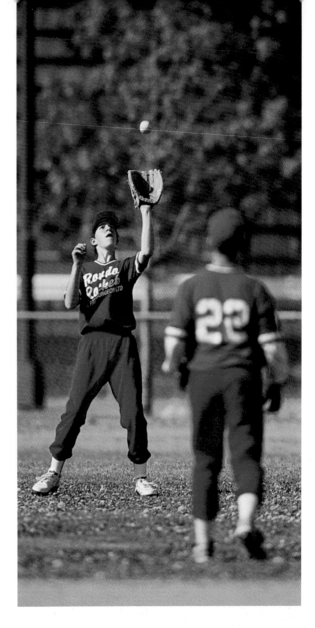

HITTING THE CUTOFF

A cutoff is any fielder who receives a throw with the intention of relaying the ball to another fielder. Here's an example that is illustrated in the diagram below:

With a runner on second base, Willie lashes a double to the left-centerfield fence. Jeremy, the centerfielder, runs to field the ball as the shortstop, Ernie, runs halfway out into the outfield. Jeremy throws the ball to Ernie. Ernie catches the ball, turns, and whips a throw to the third baseman, Mike, who is halfway between home plate and Ernie. Mike catches the ball, turns, and throws to the catcher, Brad, who catches the ball, and tags out the runner who had been on second base. Ernie and Mike were the cutoffs.

The cutoff player should be in a direct line between the fielder and the target. Because the fielder is concentrating on fielding the ball, the cutoff should yell to him or her and present a clear target.

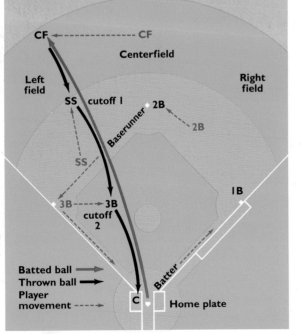

OUTFIELD

A centerfielder should be the fastest outfielder, because he or she has the most ground to cover. A rightfielder should have the strongest arm, because the longest throw an outfielder must make is the throw from rightfield to third base. A leftfielder must be the most reliable fielder, since most balls hit to the outfield will be hit to leftfield.

Learning to play baseball gives you something in common with millions of people who learned the game as children. They grew up playing and watching it and passed the game on to their children. Baseball is sometimes called America's game, but it is a popular sport in many countries. Whether you are playing inside a building on artificial grass with a synthetic ball and an aluminum bat or outside at a park on gravel with a taped-up ball and a broom handle for a bat, baseball is a great game!

BASEBALL TALK

at bat: An official attempt to hit a pitched ball. Hitting a sacrifice, being walked, or being hit by a pitch doesn't count as an at bat.

balk: An illegal motion by the pitcher when there is at least one runner on base. If the pitcher is called for a balk, the runner or runners advance one base. The three common ways to balk are dropping the ball while touching the rubber, not coming to a full stop before throwing a pitch, and stopping the delivery motion before releasing the ball.

ball: A pitch that doesn't pass through the strike zone and at which the batter doesn't swing.

base on balls: A free pass to first base, given to a batter who receives four balls before being put out by a strikeout or a fielder. Also called a walk.

batter's box: One of two 4 x 6 foot rectangles, 6 inches from both sides of home plate. The batter's boxes are marked with chalk. The batter must have one foot in one of the boxes when hitting the ball.

batting average: The number of hits a batter gets, divided by his or her official at bats, carried to three decimal places. For example, if Dave has 9 at bats and gets 3 hits, his batting average is .333—excellent!

change-up: An intentionally slow pitch that is thrown with the same motion as a fastball to fool the hitter.

curveball: A pitch thrown with a snap and twist of the pitcher's wrist. A right-handed pitcher's curve breaks from right to left; a left-hander's breaks from left to right.

double play: The act of putting out two baserunners on one play in a continuous sequence. One common double play occurs when there is a runner on first and the batter hits the ball to the second baseman. The second baseman or shortstop forces out the runner at second and throws to first to put out the batter.

error: A mistake by a fielder that results in a batter or baserunner reaching a base safely.

fastball: A pitch thrown at full speed.

fielder's choice: A decision by a fielder to throw the ball to a base other than first base in order to put out a runner already on base. The batter isn't credited with a hit even if the play isn't successful.

fly ball: A batted ball that goes high into the air above fair territory.

forceout: A situation in which a baserunner must go to the next base, but the fielder holding the ball touches the base before the baserunner. A forceout, also called a force play, can only happen at first base or when there is a runner on first base.

ground ball: A batted ball that rolls or bounces on the ground. Also called a grounder.

hit: A batted ball that causes the batter to reach base safely without benefit of an error, fielder's choice, or interference call.

home run: A batted ball that goes over the fence in fair territory to score a run for the batter's team once he or she touches all the bases. Any runners on base when the ball is hit also score. If there are three runners on base when a home run is hit, it's called a grand slam home run. An inside-the-park home run is a batted ball that is hit to such a place that the baserunner can touch all the bases before the ball is thrown home. Also called a homer.

inning: A division of the game in which each team has a turn to bat.

line drive: A hard-hit ball that travels on a straight, relatively low path.

lineup: The order in which the members of a team bat. Once the game has started, the lineup can't be changed, although substitutions are allowed. Also called the batting order.

out: The failure of a batter to reach a base safely. A team is allowed three outs in an inning.

pickoff move: A sudden throw from the

pitcher or catcher to an infielder to catch a baserunner off base.

popfly: A batted ball that goes high in the air above the infield.

putout: A play in which a defensive player stops or catches the ball to cause a batter or runner to be out.

sacrifice: A play in which the batter hits the ball and is put out but succeeds in advancing a teammate at least one base. The batter's team must have fewer than two outs.

slide: The action of a baserunner who, to avoid over-running the base or being tagged out, drops to the ground and slides to the base.

stolen base: A base that a baserunner reaches without the benefit of a hit, error, or fielder's choice.

strike: A pitch that passes through the strike zone without being hit. Also, a pitch that is hit foul when the batter has fewer than two strikes. A foul bunt is also a strike.

strikeout: An out resulting from a batter being charged with three strikes.

strike zone: The area over home plate between the batter's armpits and the top of the knees. The pitch must pass through this zone to be a strike, unless the batter swings and misses.

tag: The action of a fielder in touching a baserunner with the ball in order to put out the baserunner.

FURTHER READING

Galt, Margot Fortunato. *Up to the Plate, The All American Girls Professional Baseball League.* Minneapolis, MN: Lerner Publications, 1995.

Jordan, Pat. *Sports Illustrated Pitching: The Keys to Excellence.* New York: Sports Illustrated Books, 1993.

Kindall, Jerry. *Sports Illustrated Baseball: Play the Winning Way.* Lanham, MD: Sports Illustrated Books, 1993.

Schmidt, Mike, and Rob Ellis. *The Mike Schmidt Study: Hitting Theory, Skills and Technique.* New York: McGriff & Bell, 1994.

FOR INFORMATION

Babe Ruth League, Inc.
P. O. Box 5000
1770 Brunswick Pike
Trenton, NJ 08638
www.baberuthleague.org

Little League Baseball, Inc.
P. O. Box 3485
Williamsport, PA 17701
www.littleleague.org

U. S. A. Baseball
2160 Greenwood Avenue
Trenton, NJ 08609
www.usabaseball.com

INDEX